Endpapers The Royal Netherlands Navy frigate *Tromp* launching a Standard area air defense missile.

This book was devised and produced by Multimedia Publications (UK) Ltd

Editor: Jeff Groman
Design: John Strange and Associates
Picture Research: Military Archive & Research Services – John & Diane Moore.
Production: Arnon Orbach

ISBN 0 8317 7779 6

First published in the United States of America by Gallery Books, an imprint of W. H. Smith Publishers Inc., 112 Madison Avenue, New York, NY 10016

Originated by D. S. Colour International Ltd, London.
Printed by Cayfosa, Barcelona, Spain
Dep. Leg. B-35515 - 1984

FIGHTING SHIPS

Hugh W. Cowin

GALLERY BOOKS
An Imprint of W. H. Smith Publishers Inc.
112 Madison Avenue
New York City 10016

CONTENTS

Introduction

At the start of this century the naval cruiser represented the most awesome single weapon then in existence. On the broader front of naval warfare planning, old ideas still reigned supreme, with little in sight to threaten the type of surface action so familiar to naval officers from the days of Sir Francis Drake onwards. Indeed, virtually all of the naval warfare strategies and tactics being planned in the year 1900 would have been readily understood not only by that brilliant naval tactician of the American Civil War, Admiral David Farragut, but by the even earlier nineteenth-century British sailor, Lord Horatio Nelson. Who but the few most far-sighted naval planners and architects could possibly have guessed at the fundamental shifts to which naval warfare and its vessels would so soon be subject as the world entered the twentieth century?

Old theories under attack

The submarine was, unquestionably, the first major new naval development to be widely accepted by the world's navies in the years immediately preceding World War I. From that point on, the more conservative-minded members of the world's naval communities came under almost constant attack as new weapons of naval warfare followed one upon another, with the bitter period of 1914 through 1918 providing the major impetus. By 1918, navies throughout the world were being compelled to face the new threats of the submarine, the contact mine and the aircraft: Britain, previously one of the most conservative of the leading naval powers, introduced the world's first purpose-built aircraft carrier in the shape of HMS *Argus*.

The interwar years

In the wake of World War I, the governments of the world — and especially those of the victorious powers — were swept by a sense of remorse. This was the time to turn swords into ploughshares. Publicly, leading politicians gathered to ratify the Washington Treaty aimed at limiting the size, firepower and number of battleships possessed by any one nation, while, privately, individual governments and their naval advisers sought to find ways to get around the legislation. Britain, always reluctant to see any reduction in her naval power, worked secretly to outflank the Washington Treaty limitations and even privately encouraged others, including Japan, to do the same. As the 1920s drew to a close, the leading navies of the world, including Britain and the US, began to accept the aircraft carrier in place of the battleship as their capital naval asset.

From the early 1930s onwards the race to re-arm was spearheaded by a massive expansion in the size of the world's leading navies and nowhere more so than in the case of Germany and Japan. Germany, who had learnt more than most about the use of submarine warfare from World War I, initiated a program of submarine construction on a massive scale.

One fascinating aspect of this period centers on the mid-1930s British development of ASDIC, an acoustic aid to underwater detection, hastily fitted to most Royal Navy surface combatants and generally held to be the final solution to the submarine problem. Unfortunately for ASDIC, its limitations were soon to be pointed up as U-Boat commanders learnt to mask their movements by running on the surface, where wave noise worked very much to their advantage.

The impact of air power

The 1940s could well be characterized as the years in which the aircraft was to make a major impact on the whole shape of naval operations and the kind of warships required.

The first major air/sea actions of World War II were to be mounted by Japan with their massive surprise carrier-based air attacks on Pearl Harbor and its neighboring airfields. Within days, bomber units of the Japanese Air Force had efficiently dispatched HMS *Repulse* and HMS *Prince of Wales* to a watery grave. Within six months, it was the turn of the Japanese to suffer at the hands of air strikes from mainly US Navy carrierborne squadrons during the crucial Battle of Midway.

Meanwhile, above the vital Atlantic shipping lanes, slower, larger, less glamorous aircraft, such as the US Navy's PBY Catalina and Royal Air Force's Sunderland, were beginning to make a material contribution in the fight to combat the U-Boat.

In early August 1945, a pair of US Army Air Force B-29 Superfortresses lifted off from an Okinawa airfield, one of them carrying a single weapon that was to devastate the Japanese city of Hiroshima. This event, along with the subsequent destruction of Nagasaki by a slightly larger nuclear weapon, did more than accelerate the end of World War II; it also cast an ominous question mark over the future effectiveness of large naval task groups that had proven to be so indispensable to the conduct of the US campaign in the Pacific. For more than the next decade, major navies, such as those of the US, Britain and Soviet Russia, found themselves to be the poor orphaned cousins compared with their respective air forces when it came to share out the national defense budgetary cake.

Towards today

The re-emergence of the world's leading navies to something of their former pre-eminence was a gradual process, initiated by the US Navy's pioneering of nuclear propulsion, first for hunter/killer submarines, followed by its use in cruisers and aircraft carriers. Nuclear propulsion represented a major breakthrough in naval operational terms by providing its parent vessel with virtually unlimited range.

In the early 1960s, the US Navy closed the circle with their development of the submarine-carried intercontinental ballistic missile: a pattern to be followed by Soviet Russia, Britain, France and the Chinese Peoples' Republic. Today, with fixed, land-based ballistic missiles vulnerable to pre-emptive strike, the use of submarine-lobbed ballistic missiles has thrust the world's navies back into the forefront of national strategic nuclear-armed forces.

If the advent of nuclear propulsion and submarine-launched ballistic missiles have affected both the fortunes and the types of warships operated by the major navies over the past 25 years, the introduction of the ship-launched anti-ship missile has had an equally dramatic impact on both navies and the kind of vessels they operate worldwide. Generally, the now widespread deployment of the anti-ship missile has had the effect of equalizing the firepower available to navies large and small, with aircraft carriers and battleships having to guard against long-range missile attack from small, agile fast attack craft not as readily detectable as a larger ship.

Canadian Navy warships replenishing while underway from the fleet oiler HMCS *Protecteur* (A509).

CHAPTER 1
Submarines and Aircraft Carriers

Right HMS *Swiftsure* (S126), first of this six boat Royal Navy nuclear-powered hunter/killer class. All entered service between 1973 and 1981.

Below USS *Michigan* (SSBN727), second of this planned 15 boat Ohio class. Each of these nuclear-powered vessels carry 24 Trident ballistic missiles and is almost as long as a Virginia class cruiser.

The present generation of submarines can be grouped under two types: nucear-powered and diesel-electric powered. Within the nuclear-powered vessels, the natural categorization comprises ballistic missile launchers and hunter/killer types used to hunt other hostile submarines. For their part, the diesel-electric powered submarines' role is that of hunter/ killer primarily, with a useful secondary mission capability of attacking hostile surface vessels that may enter their patrol area. All types of submarines employed today still carry torpedoes, giving them some varying degree of both anti-submarine and anti-ship capability regardless of their primary role.

While the modern nuclear-powered submarines – and especially the intercontinental ballistic missile launchers – have tended to steal much of the limelight in recent years, it would be foolish to write off the future for the diesel-electric boats. Indeed, right now, the relatively modest but very quiet-running diesel-electric submarine is not only valued by smaller navies, but new classes of such vessels are under construction or on order for all of the world's major navies other than that of the US, but including that of the Soviets.

The power of the aircraft carrier

The aircraft carrier of today also lends itself to being grouped under two main headings: the large, conventional aircraft-catapulting types of which the US Navy operates both nuclear-powered and steam turbine driven classes, along with the much more compact jump jet and helicopter operating carriers, typified by the Royal Navy's Invincible class and Soviet Navy's Kiev class ships.

While there are those who believe that the typically large US Navy carrier provides a prime example of putting all your eggs into one basket, the between 70 and 90 plane carrying capability of each of these ships provides a single US carrier with a global range air strike capacity greater than most of world's air forces. Significantly, the Soviet Navy have recently elected to follow the same path and are currently building a 75,000 ton or more carrier of their own.

Above The lead of this French Navy class of 16 ballistic missile-carrying nuclear-powered submarines is *Le Redoutable.* Seven have been ordered.

Below The Canadian Navy's HMCS *Ojibwa* (SS72), one of three modified British-developed Oberon class diesel-electric boats.

Right HMS *Turbulent* (S114), second of this Royal Navy five boat Trafalgar class nuclear-powered hunter/killer submarines.

The *Sauro*, lead boat of this six vessel Italian Navy patrol class.

N. SAURO

Left The steam turbine-powered USS *Kitty Hawk* (CV63), first of a four carrier class that includes the modified USS *John F Kennedy* (CV67). All carry an 85 plane air group.

Lower Right An F-4 Phantom II being launched from the deck of the USS *Constellation* (CV64), a Kitty Hawk class carrier.

Upper Right USS *Carl Vinson* (CVN70), third of the six carrier Nimitz class nuclear-powered mammoths, each with a 90 plane air group.

Left HMS *Illustrious* (R06), second of this Royal Navy three ship Invincible class. Note the forward ski jump for its Sea Harriers.

Above The *Garibaldi,* first aircraft carrier to join the Italian Navy, can operate Harrier/Sea Harrier jump jets if required.

Below USS *Kitty Hawk* (CV63) steaming off Southern California in February 1979.

CHAPTER 2
Battleships, Cruisers and Destroyers

The battleship's heyday was during the late 1930s and very early 1940s, as typified by Japan's Yamato class mammoth battlewagons. Indeed, no battleship has been launched anywhere in the world since USS *Kentucky* left the slipways in January 1950, lending further support to the notion that the battleship's days were long past. However, one navy, that of the US, clung grimly to their four completed Iowa class ships, periodically bringing one or more out of mothballs to provide heavy shore bombardment support as late as 1969 off the coast of Vietnam. During the latter half of the 1970s, to many people's surprise, the US Navy revealed plans to modernize and refurbish all four battleships, the first two of which are now back in full operation.

As modernized, these veritable floating fortresses retain their big 16-inch gun batteries, now augmented by a formidable mix of Harpoon anti-ship and Tomahawk cruise missiles. Perhaps of equal importance is the fact that these heavily armed ships are also heavily armor clad, providing them with a much higher degree of surviving a strike either by bomb or missile than in the case of the far more fragile latterday warships.

The Super Power cruiser

The cruiser, once the principal surface ship employed by the large majority of navies, is rapidly becoming a luxury only affordable by the two Super Power navies of the US and Soviet Russia. Currently, there are marked differences emerging between the types of cruisers being built in the two countries, with the US opting for the relatively light Ticonderoga class anti-aircraft ships, while Soviet cruisers, of which there are a growing number of classes, tend to be more general-purpose in terms of mission and have recently started to outstrip their US contemporaries in terms of both size and weight.

The growth of the destroyers

The destroyer started life at around the turn of the last century as a relatively small, light and agile ship designed to counter the threat from the fast torpedo boat. However, since the early 1940s, the destroyer has become ever more closely associated with the anti-aircraft role. Similarly, over the past 30 years or so, the size and weight of the destroyer has crept up from around 2,500 tons to now lie in a range spanning from 4,500 tons to nearly 8,000 tons. Virtually all of the modern destroyers are gas turbine-propelled, but because of their greater weight have top speeds of around 30 knots as against the 35 or more knot capability of their World War II forebears.

Left USS *New Jersey* (BB62), the first of the four Iowa class battleships to re-enter service after modernization in December 1982.

Above USS *Ticonderoga* (CG47), first of this planned 18 ship gas turbine-powered area air defense cruiser class.

Below Right USS *Mississippi* (CGN40), third of this four ship nuclear-powered cruiser class used primarily as carrier escorts.

Left The impressively armed Italian Navy cruiser *Vittorio Veneto*, following her recent refit and looking every inch a warship.

Upper Right A Soviet Navy Kara class gas-turbine-powered cruiser. In all seven of these 9,700 ton full load displacement ships were built during the 1970s.

Lower Right Ten of these Soviet Navy Kresta II class cruisers are operated, primarily as leaders for an anti-submarine surface group.

Above USS *Elliott* (DDG967), one of the US Navy's 31 ship Spruance class gas turbine-powered guided missile destroyers.

Left The *Jean De Vienne* (D643), fourth of this ultimate seven ship French Navy destroyer class, of which *George Leygues* (D640) is the lead ship.

Far Left HMS *Glasgow* (D88), sixth and last of the Royal Navy's Type 42 Batch I Sheffield class guided missile destroyers.

Upper Left Japan's *Shirane* (DDH143), the first of this 12 ship helicopter-carrying destroyer class. Note the vast helipad area aft.
Lower Left The *Haruna* (DDH141), lead of this two ship Japanese destroyer class, which, like the Shirane class, are primarily sub killers.

Below HMCS *Iroquois* (DDH280), first of this four ship Canadian Navy destroyer class, mainly operating in the North Atlantic.

Above Two Greek operated ex-US Navy Fletcher class destroyers. More than 40 of these World War II ships remain in service with no less than ten navies.

Lower Right The US Navy Coontz class missile destroyer, USS *Luce* (DDG38). This elderly class consists of ten ships.

Lower Left The Greek operated ex-US Navy Gearing class destroyer *Toumbazis* (D215), now missile equipped, but of World War II origin. Around 45 remain in service with navies around the world.

CHAPTER 3
Frigates and Corvettes

The term frigate, for long associated in both US and French minds with the destroyer leader or light cruiser, has now generally come to be associated with an ocean-going ship, whose primary mission is to counter the submarine threat. Although still carrying the shipboard torpedoes and anti-submarine mortars of their ancestors, modern frigates place most of their operational reliance on their ship-stowed anti-submarine helicopters. As with the modern destroyers, today's frigates are almost universally gas turbine-powered, but in some cases employ diesels for fuel economy reasons when operating at lower speeds. Many of the world's frigates carry a useful anti-ship missile armament.

The versatile corvette

The corvette is generally designed for either general-purpose duties or as an anti-submarine supplement to the larger frigate. Used in great numbers by the Allied Powers during World War II's Battle of the Atlantic, the corvette appeared to drop from favor during the 1950s and 1960s, only to re-emerge in popularity since the beginning of the 1970s. As endurance, rather than high dash speeds, are a prime design feature of most modern corvettes, the primary propulsion usually chosen is the diesel, although both US and Dutch corvette constructors have employed gas turbines for ships supplied to Saudi Arabia and Indonesia respectively. Although still far from common practise, the latest Italian-developed Esmeraldas class corvettes of 700 tons are capable of deploying a respectably-sized AB212ASW helicopter from their elevated aft helipad platform. Many modern corvettes carry anti-ship missiles.

Center Right The *Tromp* (F801), lead of this two ship Royal Netherlands Navy frigate class, seen in her customary role as task group leader.

Lower Right The *Banckert* (F810), the fourth of the 12 Dutch-built and operated Kortenaer class frigates.

Above HMS *Beaver* (F93), second of the Royal Navy's six ship stretched Batch II Broadsword class gas turbine-powered frigates.

Right and Below Forward and aft views of HMS *Broadsword* (F88), the first of four Type 22 Royal Navy frigates. Note the forward and aft mounted Seawolf rapid response, close-in anti-aircraft missile launchers and Westland Lynx anti-submarine helicoper, one of two carried by each ship.

Upper Left The Italian lead of class gas turbine-powered frigate *Lupo* (F564) and her three sister ships were all delivered between 1977 and 1980.

Upper Right Italy's *Maestrale* (F570), first of her navy's new eight ship gas turbine-powered, 34 knot anti-submarine frigates.

Below Italy's Lupo class is the most widely exported of all modern frigates, with 14 sales. Shown here is the Venezuelan Navy's *Jose Felix Ribas* (F26).

Top HMS *Amazon* (F169), lead of this original eight ship Royal Navy frigate class, two of which were lost to heavy Argentinian air attacks while serving in Falklands Sound.

Left Not normally operated in such close company are these three US Navy Sperry class frigates comprising from front to rear USS *Jack Williams* (F24), USS *Antrim* (F20) and USS *Sperry* (F0 7).

206

Left The Canadian frigate HMCS *Sauguenag* (F206), eldest of this six ship helicopter-carrying St. Laurent class.

Above Britain's Royal Navy operates eight Leander class frigates modified to mount the Ikara anti-submarine missile, including HMS *Aurora* (F10) shown here.

Below KNS *Trondheim* (F302), third of the Royal Norwegian Navy five ship Oslo class frigates.

Above The *Liberal* (F43) is the fourth of Brazil's six ship Niteroi class frigates designed in Britain, where four were built.

Right and Left Two informative views of the Federal German Navy's lead of class frigate *Bremen* (F207). The Bremen class uses the Dutch-developed Kortenaer class hull and same general layout, but employs US rather than British gas turbines as its prime propulsion. Six ships have been completed, but more may be ordered.

F354

508

Above The Royal Danish Navy operates three of these Niels Juel class corvettes. Shown here is the lead ship, F354.

Lower Left The Soviet Navy's sleek and low profiled 17 ship Krivak I class frigate is gas turbine-powered.

Lower Right The *Cazadora* (F35), fifth of Spain's eight Descubierta class corvettes. Egypt and Morocco also operate this type.

Left The third of the D'Estienne D'Orves class, *Drogou* (F783). Argentina operates three of these ships as their Drummond class.

Right The *D'Estienne D'Orves* (F781), lead ship of this 17 corvette French Navy class, looses one of its Exocet anti-ship missiles.

Below Despite its small size, *Esmeraldas* (CM11), lead of this six Ecuadorian corvette class, built in Italy, can operate a sizeable anti-submarine helicopter from its aft helipad.

F781

CHAPTER 4
Fast Attack and Patrol Vessels

The small, fast and agile fast attack craft has been around in one form or another since the 1890s. Up to the mid-1960s, the primary offensive armament of such craft had been the 21-inch heavyweight torpedo employed as an anti-surface ship weapon. Thanks largely to the Soviet-led development of the relatively lightweight ship-launched anti-ship missile, the current generation of fast attack craft have been given the same firepower potency as that of warships many times their size. Historically, Germans have tended to excel in the design and development of these types and it should therefore come as no surprise to find the West German boatbuilders maintaining dominance in the fast attack craft markets worldwide. Interestingly, the 1960s and early 1970s courtship between the fast attack craft designer and the gas turbine engine appears to be on the wane, with most of the more recently designed craft exploiting the fuel economies offered by the new breed of diesel engines now available.

The role of the patrol vessel

The patrol vessel category covers a variety of ships and craft ranging from the very modern breed of 1,200 ton ocean-going patrol and fishery protection vessels, to 30 or 40 ton inshore patrol boats employed in river or harbor policing duties.

Born out of the mid-1970s internationally agreed extension of national territorial waters limits out to 200 nautical miles from shore, Britain was the first to field a specialized solution to the emerging market for economic but effective offshore patrol vessels in the shape of the Royal Navy's Island class. Following on from the Island class, the Royal Navy has taken delivery of two somewhat larger Castle class ships and is in the course of accepting five Peacock class patrol vessels for use in Hong Kong waters. Spain is another nation that has produced a new offshore patrol vessel, in this case equipped with a helicopter platform aft, and has sold five of this class to Argentina and another six to Mexico.

USS *Hercules* (PHM2), the second of this five craft US Navy missile-armed Pegasus fast attack hydrofoil class.

Left One of the Egyptian Navy's six craft, missile-equipped Ramadan class at speed.

Below The Omani Navy's *Dhofar* (B10), first of the three craft Province class designed and built in Britain.

Upper Right A French-built Combattante III class missile craft, this particular vessel being the Greek *Simaiforos Kavalouthis* (P24).

Lower Right The *Dogan* (P340), lead of this Turkish Navy operated class of Lurssen-designed Type FPB57 missile craft.

Left One of the ten Federal German Navy missile armed, Lurssen-designed Type 143A fast attack craft.

P542
P542

Upper The *Hammer* (P542), one of ten Willemoes class fast attack craft belonging to the Royal Danish Navy.

Lower Two Swedish Navy Spica class fast attack craft, of which there are six, demonstrating their impressive turn of speed.

Above The Norwegians operate six Snogg class fast attack craft, this one being *Rapp* (P981), the second to be built.

Left The *Skudd* (P967), one of the 19 Storm class remaining in Norwegian service, seen unleashing a Penguin anti-ship missile.

Right The *Terne* (P988), third of this Royal Norwegian Navy 14 craft Hawk class firing a Penguin anti-ship missile.

P 981

P988

Above and Right Italy operates seven of these OTOMAT anti-ship missile-armed Sparviero class fast attack hydrofoils developed under a joint programme with the US. Shown here are the lead craft *Sparviero* (P420) and *Nibbio* (P421).

Left Bahrain's *P11,* second of this two craft Lurssen FPB38 design class, each armed with two single 40mm Breda/Bofors guns.

P258
LEEDS CASTLE
P258

Right Argentina ordered five of these Spanish designed and built Halcon class patrol vessels. Seen here is the lead Argentinian ship, *Mantilla* (GC24).

Left The Royal Navy's HMS *Leeds Castle* (P258), lead ship of this two patrol vessel class.

Below HMS *Peacock* (P239), first of this latest Royal Navy five patrol vessel class is fitted with a rapid fire OTO-Melara 76mm gun.

CHAPTER 5
Support Vessels

This chapter covers a relatively wide variety of non-combatant vessels ranging from the vast, latterday US Navy's Tarawa class assault ships, through the vital underway replenishers to minehunters and landing craft: all of which play a largely unsung but crucial role in the overall scheme of naval operations.

The modern assault ship, typified by the Tarawa class in the US and the Soviet's Ivan Rogov class vessels, is a far cry from the virtually standard commercial cargo and troopship designs employed during World War II. All modern assault ships carry a sizable helicopter-operating platform from which to vertically dispatch their marine infantry, while the below deck space carries a vast volume of fighting equipment, ammunition and sustaining stores. Most modern assault ships are equipped with a floodable well deck astern, enabling them to house and subsequently disembark up to tank carrying-sized landing craft.

Minesweepers and their successors
The present-day mine countermeasures vessel has also come a long way from the relatively simple minesweepers of World War II. Threatened as they are by the numerous ways in which a modern mine can be triggered, today's minehunters can still be operated in pairs or teams to clear a channel through a sown field of conventional mines, but need more than one trick up their sleeve to counter the more clever devices that are becoming ever more prevalent, thanks largely to advances in mine electronics. To combat such weapons, the modern minehunter is designed to offer the minimum magnetic, sound and pressure indications of its presence during operation. Equipped with high-definition sonar, the minehunter slowly advances to within safe range of an unidentified underwater target, which is then inspected at close quarters by a small, remotely-controlled submersible launched from the minehunter. If the target does turn out to be some form of mine, the submersible leaves a destructive

charge close to the mine and withdraws back to its mother ship, which then triggers the charge and so destroys the mine. If for any reason it is needed to retrieve the mine for subsequent inspection, the minehunter dispatches a team of naval divers to bring the device aboard.

Significantly, the US Navy, which has tended to neglect its surface mine countermeasures assets over the past 30 or so years, has now embarked on two major minehunter programmes: one to counter the deepwater, anti-submarine mine; the other to combat shallow seabed or tethered mines.

Tanker support

The part played by the underway replenisher or fleet oiler in modern naval operations any distance from base cannot be overstated, for without these vital fuel and supply-laden workhorses, the tactical operational radius of a task group's action could be counted in hundreds, rather than thousands, of miles. Indeed, as the recent experience of the Royal Navy's South Atlantic Task Force showed, no British repossession of the Falklands could even have been contemplated without the tanker support provided by the ships of the Royal Fleet Auxiliary. Significantly, after many years of relying upon their merchant tanker and cargo-carrying fleet to resupply active naval units, the Soviets have in recent years turned to the development of naval replenishers to help extend the sea legs of their fighting ships.

All too often overlooked by armchair strategists, the landing craft clearly comes into its own when the need arises to put troops ashore or resupply beach-head forces with loads too heavy to be ferried in by helicopter. Ironically, despite Britain's pioneering development of the air cushion or hovercraft, it was the Soviet Navy that was to produce a family of air cushion landing craft, the largest of which can speed 220 troops or a mix of troops and main battle tanks over the water and far beyond the beach at over 40 miles per hour.

Left Easily mistaken for an aircraft carrier, USS *Peleliu* (LHA5) is, in fact, the last of the US Navy five vessel Tarawa class assault ships, each of which can transport nearly 2,000 marines and their equipment.

Below Malaysia operates two of these Sri Indera Lakti class multi-purpose support ships. Shown here is the lead, A1503.

Below The Italian Navy's *Lerici* (M5550), the first of this new minehunter class also ordered by Indonesia, Nigeria and Malaysia, accounting for 20 sales by late 1984.

Upper Right The *Eridan* (M641), lead vessel of this French Navy minehunter class, also operated by the Belgium and Dutch navies. The three navies plan to purchase 40 such vessels.

Lower Right HMS *Cattistock* (M31), leading HMS *Ledbury* (M30), two of the Royal Navy's Hunt class minehunters. 11 of these very capable ships have been ordered by late 1984.

M641

M31

Upper Left HMS *Waveney* (M2003), the first of this 12 ship deep water minesweeper class being delivered to the Royal Navy.

Lower Left The fleet oiler HMCS *Provider* (A0508) serves with the Canadian Navy's West Coast group.

Upper Right The Japanese minelayer *Soya* (MMC951) can lay six lanes of mines simultaneously.

Center Right The *Var* (A608), third of this French Navy four ship Durance class underway replenisher, also ordered by Australia.

Right Japan's *Narushima* (M657), ninth of the Hatsushima class minehunters. 13 had been ordered by early 1984.

L3532

RFA *Sir Lamorak* (L3532) is operated by Britain's Royal Fleet Auxiliary as a roll-on, roll-off bulk cargo carrier.

710

Above One of the six British Hovercraft Wellington class patrol/landing craft sold to Iran prior to the overthrow of the Shah.

Far Left Two Aist class Soviet Navy air cushion landing craft disembarking their cargo of T-62 main battle tanks.

Left A Soviet Navy Aist class landing craft. Clearly visible are the aircraft-style propellers used for propulsion.

Overleaf The Dutch fleet replenisher, HNLMS *Zuiderkruis* (A832).

A832

Picture Credits

Canadian Armed Forces 3, 21, 30 **CMN** 43 top **Hugh Cowin** 5 top, 7 bottom, 9, 14, 15 bottom right, 16, 20 top, 20 bottom, 23, 24-25, 26-27, 31 top, 36-37, 42, 44-45 top, 48, 52-53, 54-55, 55 top, 56 bottom, 57 top, 58-59, Bazan 35, 51, Bremer Vulkan 32 bottom, 33, 53, CNR 27, Crown Copyright 18, 25 bottom, S.F. Gilman 8, Hall Russell 50, Hellenic Navy 22, 22-23, Italian Navy 26, Lurssen 43 bottom, Ministry of Defence 34, Novosti 60, R.N. Photo 28-29 top, Sovaernets Material Kommando 34-35, US Department of Defense 6 top and bottom, Vosper Thornycroft (UK) Ltd 55 bottom **Daily Telegraph** front cover, back cover **E.C.P. Armées** 5 bottom, 3 bottom **Hall Russell** 50-51 **McClancy Collection** end papers, title page, 62-63 **Maritime Nationale, France** 19 bottom **M.A.R.S** 4, 6 centre, 8-9, 15 top, 38-39, 40-41, 48-49, 49, 57 bottom, Crown Copyright 7 top, 12, 13 top, 25 top, Royal Norwegian Navy 31 bottom, 46, 46-47, 47, Royal Swedish Navy 44-45 bottom, US Navy 10-11, 11 bottom, 13 bottom, 15 bottom left, 17 bottom, 19 top, 28-29 bottom, 61, Vosper Thornycroft (UK) Ltd 40 **Newport News Shipbuilding** Chris Oxley 11 top **Rolls Royce** 60-61 **Royal Netherlands Navy** 24 top and bottom **US Department of Defense** 17 top **Vosper Thornycroft (UK) Ltd** 32 top.

F 80